IT'S BRAVE TO BE KIND

A KINDNESS STORY AND ACTIVITY BOOK FOR CHILDREN

WRITTEN BY
NATASHA DANIELS

ILLUSTRATED BY
ELA SMIETANKA

ROCKRIDGE
PRESS

Dear Caregivers and Educators,

Kindness, compassion, and empathy are skills, and not all children are proficient in them naturally. Like other developmental abilities, these skills grow when caregivers and educators foster and model them. When kindness, compassion, and empathy grow, a child's emotional intelligence expands.

Emotional intelligence is more important today than ever before. In a world filled with diversity and difference, it is our job to teach our children to open their hearts and minds to others, and to embrace the uniqueness in all of us.

As caregivers and educators, we can take an active role in developing these skills. We can use books like this one, sharing stories that weave together concepts of empathy, kindness, and acceptance. We can model kindness and empathy, because our children are always watching. As role models for our children, we need to ask ourselves:

- Am I showing acceptance and kindness in my daily interactions?
- How do I talk about people who are different?
- How do I treat people who are different?
- Do I speak up and stand up for those who need support?

This book is not meant to be read passively. Instead, it's meant to be a catalyst for deeper conversation. You can encourage this by expanding upon the themes and messages in this book.

Acceptance

In this story, the main character, Alex, likes being different, and she embraces differences. When a new student arrives, she not only accepts him but is also excited to learn about his culture, his language, and his family.

Some kids may get nervous around people who are different than them. They may not know what to expect or think. As caregivers and educators, we can teach kids that "different" doesn't equal "bad." We can teach children that our differences offer a unique learning experience. As you read this book, you can ask your child:

1. Have you ever met anyone who seemed different?
2. In what ways were they different?
3. What were your feelings toward them?
4. What did you learn from them?

IT'S BRAVE TO BE KIND

Empathy

In this story, the main character, Alex, senses that the new student is uncomfortable. She puts herself in his shoes and imagines how it would feel to be at a new school and not know English well.

Not all kids have an innate ability to put themselves in someone else's shoes. We can develop this ability by strengthening a child's awareness of the emotional states of those around them. Here are two ways you can do this:

1. When reading books, pause and ask your child to guess how the main characters feel at that moment.
2. When in a public area, ask your child to guess the feelings of people around you. You can make this a game between the two of you.

Mind-Body Connection

Throughout this book, the main character gets an upset feeling in her stomach when she witnesses other students being unkind to the new student.

We can help children stay in touch with their feelings by teaching them that their bodies will give them clues. Being aware of this mind-body connection is a huge asset. It helps guide a child to do what "feels" right. Ask your child:

1. When you feel nervous, where do you feel it in your body?
2. When was the last time you felt that way in your body?
3. What do you think your body was trying to tell you?

Being True to Yourself

A big message in this book is teaching kids to be true to themselves. The main character loves meeting new and different people. She is given a choice to do what the other children want her to do (not play with the new student) or to do what she wants to do.

Teaching kids to be independent thinkers will create empathetic leaders, not followers. You can ask your child:

1. Have you ever done something that the rest of the group wasn't doing?
2. What are some things you love?
3. What things are important to you? You can introduce the concept of values by asking, "Is it important for you to be nice? Considerate?"

Doing What Feels Right

At the end of the story, the main character does what feels right to her. It didn't feel good to watch the other kids being mean to the new student. It didn't feel good to not play with him because the other kids said she shouldn't. She was brave and did what felt right.

We can teach kids that doing what feels right is important. We also want to recognize that it can be a scary and brave thing to do. You can ask your child:

1. Can you think of a time when you felt someone was being treated badly?
2. What did you do?
3. What can you do when this happens?

I hope you and your child enjoy reading this book!

HI, KIDS!

Do you know what kindness is? Of course you do! But did you know there is so much more to kindness than being nice? In this story, you will read about a girl named Alex who is kind. Being kind means she is also accepting, caring, and brave.

What does it mean to be accepting? In this story, Alex isn't afraid of people who are different. In fact, she loves to meet people who are different from her.

Alex is also caring, and she can imagine how other people might feel.

Alex is brave. Even though she is afraid to stick up for someone else, she does it, and it feels good!

As you read this story, think of the ways that you are already kind and brave. Then imagine ways to start being even more kind, caring, and brave at home, in school, and when you are out and about!

Alex woke up and reached her arms up high, as far as they could go. She got out of bed and stretched her legs, taking giant steps to the kitchen.

This was different from yesterday, when Alex jumped out of bed and hopped to the kitchen.

Everybody wakes up and gets out of bed, thought Alex. *It's perfectly ordinary.*

But I do it a different way every day.

Alex loved to be different.

Every morning, Alex ate cereal a differe
she poured tea over her cereal instea

She used her hands to talk to her d
know sign language. *Maybe we ca*
thought Alex.

When Alex said goodbye to her family, even her
goodbyes were different.

She gave her little brother a high five. She gave
her mom a bear hug and growled a little.

Alex rode the bus to school. She looked out the window.

Every day, she saw the same buildings, trees, and sidewalks.
She noticed when things were different.

The dog walker she saw every day had only five dogs today.

Yesterday, there were seven dogs.

At school, Alex noticed that something was *very* different.

Her classroom was quiet. Instead of hearing everyone talking and laughing, she heard silence.

There was a new boy sitting in the back of the classroom.

Who is that boy? wondered Alex. *Where did he come from?*

The other kids asked him what his name was.

"I, Jon," he said. He spoke with an accent.

"Where are you from?" they asked.

The boy looked confused and said, "I, Jon."

The kids in the class started to laugh.

One kid laughed the loudest. It was Greg.

Alex wondered, *Why are they laughing?*

The new boy *did* sound different.

But what was wrong with different?

Ms. Jen came in and hushed the class. She spoke with excitement.

"We have a new student in our class. His name is Jon. Jon knows Spanish because he is from another country where people speak Spanish.

"He will learn English here with us. Please help him get used to the class."

Alex was excited to meet someone from another country.

She wondered what foods his family ate and how far Jon had traveled to get here.

Alex liked making new friends.

Ms. Jen told everyone to take out their math homework.

Alex pulled out her homework but didn't look at it. She looked at Jon one more time.

Her heart sank. *Why is he crying?*

Greg was still staring at Jon and whispering to the other students.

Alex felt yucky in her stomach.

It was the same feeling Alex got when Greg said she had cooties and no one wanted to play with her.

Ms. Jen hushed the class again. She turned to write on the board.

As soon as Ms. Jen faced away from the class, Greg threw a paper airplane at Jon's head.

Everyone laughed except Alex.

Alex wondered if she should say something. What could she do? Greg could be so mean.

Before Alex decided what to do, Ms. Jen turned around and gave the class a stern look.

"That's not how we treat new students!" she said.

Being new is hard, Alex thought. *It was hard for me when I was new last year. It must be even harder if you don't know how to speak English yet.*

Greg is being mean, and that makes it harder.

Jon looked up from his desk and saw Alex.

Alex smiled and gave him a small wave.

Jon smiled and gave her a small wave back.

Time flew by as Alex imagined all the questions she wanted to ask Jon.

He probably had so many stories to tell!

At recess, Alex searched the playground for Jon.
She couldn't wait to play with him!

Alex almost gave up, but then she saw two feet.

They were sticking out from behind a nearby tree.

She saw kids on the other side of the tree teasing Jon.

Alex felt a little sick. It was that yucky feeling in her stomach.

Her face got warm with anger.

"Greg! Stop being so mean to Jon!" Alex said.

Greg turned away from Jon and looked at Alex.

"Mind your own business!" Greg yelled.

Alex turned to Jon and said,

"Jon, do you want to play with me?"

He didn't say a word, but he
looked happy.

Greg started to laugh, and the other kids joined in.

"If you play with *him*, forget about EVER playing with us."

Greg was the boss of the playground. If Alex didn't play with Greg, maybe no one would play with her.

She thought about what to do.

"We don't want to play with you anyway," Greg said to Alex. "You're too different. Your hair is weird."

Alex's hands shot up to her head. She touched her new haircut. It *was* different. No one in her class had hair like hers.

"I like my new hair," said Alex.

Alex started to think. *I like Jon*, she thought. *I want to play with him. I want to hear him speak Spanish. Maybe I can learn how to speak it!*

I want to ask Jon what his country was like, and what foods he ate there.

I wonder, does he have a sister? Does she go to our school?

Alex took a deep breath. She was about to do something brave.

Alex reached out her hand to Jon and said,
"Jon, do you want to play with me?"

"Si!" he said with a big smile.

"Does that mean yes?" asked Alex.

"Sí, yes," said Jon, nodding.

Greg's face turned red. He said to the other kids,
"Come on, let's go!"

Alex told Jon she was sorry the other kids were treating him in a mean way.

She hoped he understood, even if he didn't know English very well.

She pointed to the soccer field, and they went to play.

Jon was good at soccer. Very good.

He showed Alex how they played in his country.

He showed her how to dribble the ball from knee to knee.

Soon, a few kids stopped playing with Greg and ran to the field.

"Can we play with you?" they asked.

"Sure!" said Alex.

One by one, all the kids left Greg and ran to the field.

It was fun trying to bounce the ball on their knees.
And it was fun to watch everyone try.

Everyone except Greg.

Alex wondered where Greg was—and then she saw him.

His two feet stuck out from behind the tree.

"Are you okay?" asked Alex.

"Why do you care?" said Greg. "Go away!"

But Alex didn't go away.

"You aren't always nice, Greg, but I don't want you to be upset. Everyone's feelings are important," she said.

Greg stood up.

"It isn't fair that everyone left. We were having a good time, and you took them away," he said sadly.

"You don't have to be the boss all the time," said Alex, who was feeling very confident.

"But he doesn't speak English," said Greg.

Alex laughed. "We don't speak Spanish. You don't have to speak the same language to play with a soccer ball."

"We're just trying something different," said Alex. "We're learning to bounce balls on our knees. Jon is showing us how. He's nice. Come and play."

Alex wanted to go back to the field and have fun. She had invited Greg to play, and it was time for her to go back.

"Hey, wait!" yelled Greg.

Greg picked up a ball and kicked it hard at Jon,
who stopped it with his two feet.

Jon flipped the ball up and kicked it back to Greg.

Jon was great at soccer, but Greg was good, too.

Alex noticed that she didn't have that yucky feeling in her stomach anymore.

She was happy she had listened to her heart.

She was happy she had been brave.

Today was a different kind of day, thought Alex, *and that made it perfect!*

PUTTING KINDNESS INTO PRACTICE

KINDNESS STARTS WITH YOURSELF

Kindness isn't only about how you treat others. It is also about how you treat YOURSELF! You shouldn't say anything to yourself that you wouldn't say to your best friend. After all, your very, very best friend should be you!

Sometimes we forget to treat ourselves kindly. This can be even more tricky when we mess up, get in trouble, or feel sad.

Here is a list of things you can do when you need to calm down:

- **Color**
- **Blow bubbles**
- **Spend time with your pet**
- **Talk to someone you love**
- **Make a list of things you like about yourself**
- **Close your eyes and create your own cool world**
- **Listen to music**
- **Have a dance party**

KINDNESS CHALLENGES

Are you ready to take some Kindness Challenges? Here are six to get you started. See if you can come up with some of your own as well!

School Kindness Challenges:

- Say hello to someone in your class you've never talked to before.
- Write a short note saying something kind to someone in your class.
- Ask someone to play with you at recess who doesn't have anyone to play with.

Home Kindness Challenges:

- Hug your brother, sister, or parents.
- Write a thank-you letter to your parents for something they did for you.
- Offer to help your parents with something around the house.

Kindness Questions to Ask Yourself:

- What did you do to help someone this week?
- How do you feel when you help another person?
- How do you think the other person feels when you help?

It's magical the way kindness can grow. Being kind and sharing kindness makes other people want to do it, too. Before you know it, you'll see kindness growing all around.

Further Resources for Caregivers and Educators

For Families: 7 Tips for Raising Caring Kids

MCC.GSE.Harvard.edu/resources-for-families/7-tips-raising-caring-kids

Beyond Our Neighbors: A Curriculum for Expanding Empathy and Compassion to "Others"

DoingGoodTogether.org/lessons/beyond-our-neighbors

Doing Good Together

DoingGoodTogether.org

Intentionally Raising Kind Kids

CoffeeAndCarpool.com/raising-kind-kids-2

Just Be Kind Club

DoingGoodTogether.org/lessons/just-be-kind-club

Making Caring Common Project

MCC.GSE.Harvard.edu

The Raising Kind Kids Movement (Facebook Group)

Facebook.com/groups/1423686061095420

About the Author

Natasha Daniels is a child anxiety and OCD therapist and a mom to three kids. She is the author of *How to Parent Your Anxious Toddler*, *Anxiety Sucks: A Teen Survival Guide*, and *Social Skills Activities for Kids*. She is also the creator of ATParentingSurvival.com, the host of *The AT Parenting Survival Podcast*, and the creator of the YouTube channel *Ask the Child Therapist*.

About the Illustrator

Ela Smietanka is an illustrator from Poland. She graduated from the Academy of Fine Arts in Krakow and works as a freelancer. Ela lives in Krakow with her husband, two sons, and a cat and enjoys Nordic walking in the mountains.

TO THE REAL ALEX,
WHO IS ONE OF THE BRAVEST, KINDEST KIDS I KNOW!

For general information on our other products and services or to obtain technical support, please contact our Customer Care Department within the U.S. at (866) 744-2665, or outside the U.S. at (510) 253-0500.

Rockridge Press publishes its books in a variety of electronic and print formats. Some content that appears in print may not be available in electronic books, and vice versa.

Interior and Cover Designer: Stephanie Sumulong

Art Producer: Samantha Ulban

Editor: Barbara J. Isenberg

Production Editor: Rachel Taenzler

Illustrations by © 2020 Ela Smietanka. Author photo courtesy of © Paul M. Hill. Illustrator photo courtesy of © Joanna Wysmyk.

ISBN: Print 978-1-64611-835-9 | eBook 978-1-64739-381-6

R0

CPSIA information can be obtained
at www.ICGtesting.com
Printed in the USA
JSHW050339311021
19793JS00002B/4

9 781646 118359